Most people with real wealth — earned through businesses, careers, or real estate — are handed the same cookie-cutter investment advice as everyone else: a 60/40 portfolio, passive index funds, and vague talk about "time in the market." But real investors don't operate that way. They don't have time for underperformance. They need real income, tax-efficiency, and dynamic strategies that adapt to the market and their lives.

This book is about what actually works. Not in theory. Not in a vacuum. But in the real world.

-Alexis Buchholz
Managing Partner, BFG Wealth Management

How to Build
Portfolios
That Actually Work

How to Build Portfolios That Actually Work

For Investors Who Want Growth, Income, and Tax Efficiency

Alexis Buchholz

BFG WEALTH MANAGEMENT

BFG Wealth Management
3838 Oak Lawn Ave Ste 1000
Dallas, TX 75219

Email: info@bfgwm.com
Website: www.bfgwm.com

Printed in the United States of America
ISBN: 979-8-218-77503-2
First Edition

Cover and interior design by Shahla Buchholz
Published by BFG Wealth Management

Dedication

To Jarrette:
My best friend since middle school,
who didn't care about portfolios or planning,
but somehow had life figured out better than most.
You showed me what it means to love people well,
and to live a life that matters.
Miss you every day.

Acknowledgments

To my wife, Shahla: Thank you for your patience, your quiet strength, and your grace in living alongside my intensity. You've given me the space to build, to focus, and to pour myself into my work, all while anchoring our family with love and stability.

To my four boys, Soheil, Mikheil, Ayden, and Kyren: Thank you for letting me chase big ideas while reminding me, every day, what truly matters. Your curiosity, humor, and energy keep me grounded and inspired. This book is one way I hope to build something lasting, for you and because of you.

To the clients I've had the privilege of serving: Thank you for your trust, your honesty, and the chance to walk alongside you as you build lives of purpose and impact. You've shaped how I think, how I advise, and ultimately, how this book was written.

Contents

Introduction: The Problem with "Conventional" Investing

If you're like most high-earning professionals or business owners, you've worked hard, sacrificed, saved diligently, and made smart financial decisions to accumulate your wealth. But when it comes time to invest that wealth, you're handed the same generic advice as everyone else: "Just stick with a 60/40 portfolio," or "Buy the index and forget it."

That kind of advice might work for someone just starting out or saving a few hundred dollars a month. But it doesn't work for you. It doesn't consider your tax situation, your cash flow needs, your business interests, your real estate holdings, or the fact that you can't afford to watch your hard-earned capital underperform for a decade or more.

Most portfolios fail to perform not because markets are unpredictable, but because they're built without purpose. They're designed for the average investor, not the actual investor. They're built by institutions trying to scale advice, not by professionals trying to deliver specific outcomes. Too often, they also ignore the very things that matter most: income, taxes, timing, and flexibility.

This book is different. It's not about theory. It's not about beating the market. It's about building a portfolio that works in the real world, for real investors. It's for people who want growth but understand the value of income. For those who are focused on after-tax results, not just pre-tax potential. For investors who don't want a sales pitch, just a strategy that works.

1

In this book, you'll find the same frameworks I use with clients at my firm every day. Strategies that blend income generation, thematic investing, tax-aware design, and real estate integration into portfolios that are practical, resilient, and goal-driven.

If you're tired of vague advice and ready to take control of your portfolio with a clearer strategy, this book is for you.

1:
Why Most Portfolios Don't Work

We're not here to throw everything out. We're here to fix what's broken and keep what works. Once your portfolio fits your real life, it'll finally work for your real goals.

If you've ever felt like your investment portfolio doesn't truly reflect your life, you're not imagining it. Most portfolios fail to perform not because they're completely wrong, but because they're completely generic. They're designed to be simple, scalable, and easy to manage... for the advisor. Not for you and your own situation.

The conventional approach relies heavily on asset allocation models created decades ago. These models assume that you're a retiree, that you have no outside income, and that your tax situation is either irrelevant or immovable. They ignore the fact that many high-net-worth investors earn substantial income, own businesses, or have meaningful real estate holdings that already carry risk, cash flow, and tax consequences.

They Ignore Taxes, Liquidity, and Timing

The average portfolio treats a dollar earned as a dollar kept. But you know that's not true. Capital gains taxes, interest income, passive losses, depreciation recapture – all of these can drastically change the real return of your investments. Timing matters as well. Are you retiring in five years? Buying a building in two? Selling a business in one? That context should reshape everything about how your capital is deployed.

Real Case: Preparing for a Business Sale With Smart Tax Planning

A client of ours was preparing to sell his business in two years, yet his previous advisor had him 80% in long-term growth stocks with high embedded capital gains. No thought was given to his tax bracket post-sale, or how he could benefit from tax-loss harvesting or asset location strategies before and after the transition. When we redesigned his allocation, we balanced growth with short-term income generation and created liquidity buffers tailored to his exit timeline. It wasn't magic. It was just thoughtful planning.

They Use Outdated Allocation Models
The 60/40 model – the portfolio construction standard for decades – is increasingly misaligned with today's market realities. Interest rates are volatile, inflation is sticky, and global markets are more connected and reactive than ever before. Static models don't reflect your flexibility, your income options, or your evolving risk tolerance.

We see this all too often with clients in their 50s who are still earning well into the high six figures but are being placed into retirement-mode portfolios. The result? Missed opportunities for capital growth in favor of fixed income that they don't even need yet. The portfolio becomes sluggish, not safe.

They Treat Every Client Like a Retiree
Ironically, many firms use "retirement planning" as the default investment lens. But what if you're still earning? What if your real estate covers your income needs? What if your goal is capital growth or estate optimization, not a 4% withdrawal rate? Your life path needs to dictate your investment design, not the other way around.

Real Case: Reducing Tax Drag Through Smarter Allocation

We developed a plan for a couple who had over $4 million in liquid assets and significant rental income from a real estate portfolio. Their previous portfolio was entirely structured around producing income they didn't need, creating unnecessary tax drag and duplication. By reallocating toward tax-efficient growth positions and integrating their real estate cash flow into their broader financial model, we reduced taxes and aligned the portfolio with their actual goals.

They Don't Integrate Your Whole Financial Picture

Your real estate, your private equity, your business ownership – these aren't side notes. They're core parts of your financial life. A portfolio that ignores them isn't neutral; it's blind. Effective portfolios integrate these realities. They adjust for concentration risk, create balance where needed, and leverage what you already own to improve your outcomes.

You might have $500k in a brokerage account and another $2 million in real estate equity. If your advisor only sees the $500k, you'll likely get advice that ignores most of your actual balance sheet. Risk may be duplicated. Liquidity may be lacking. And your tax efficiency will be accidental, at best.

They Ignore Tax Brackets and Asset Location

One of the most overlooked drivers of portfolio underperformance is the misalignment between where assets are held and how they're taxed. For example, holding municipal bonds in a Roth IRA provides no tax benefit but wastes valuable tax-free space. On the other hand, placing high-yield taxable bonds in a brokerage account can create unnecessary tax drag that can easily be avoided.

Real investors benefit from understanding where their investments live. A growth stock with no dividend is often better in a taxable account for long-term capital gain treatment, while ordinary income-producing assets can be sheltered in retirement accounts. Strategic asset location isn't complicated, it's just rarely done well.

They Confuse Diversification with Duplication

True diversification is about spreading risk, not repeating it across accounts. We've reviewed countless portfolios where investors hold a dozen mutual funds, ETFs, and separately managed accounts, believing that more holdings equals more safety. But once you break it down, many of those funds are chasing the exact same handful of stocks.

This kind of redundancy is especially common with passive investing. Take the S&P 500, for example. Most people assume it's a broad representation of the 500 largest companies in the U.S. economy. But that's not entirely accurate. While it does include 500 companies, the index is weighted by market capitalization, which means the largest companies dominate the index's performance. In fact, just the top ten holdings now account for nearly a third of the total weight of the S&P 500. These names are familiar: Apple, Microsoft, Amazon, Nvidia, Alphabet, and a few others.

When you own multiple index funds or mutual funds that track the S&P 500 or similar benchmarks, you're not adding variety. You're doubling and tripling down on the same names. You may have twenty different fund names on your statement, but under the surface, a huge portion of your exposure is concentrated in the same corner of the market.

This kind of hidden concentration risk is common even among high-net-worth investors. It often goes unnoticed because statements look diversified. But when markets shift, the overlap becomes obvious — usually in the form of sharper drawdowns than expected.

The solution is not necessarily to abandon index funds or passive strategies. It's to be intentional. A thoughtful allocation strategy recognizes where overlap exists and seeks to reduce it, either by consolidating holdings or by building complementary positions that serve different purposes.

For example, instead of owning five large-cap growth funds with nearly identical top holdings, we might consolidate to one core equity fund, then add selective exposure to small caps, value stocks, or international markets. We also design around goals. If the objective is income, then we build with that in mind. If it's capital growth, then we want assets that aren't just riding the same wave.

Diversification is not about quantity. It's about alignment. When you understand how your portfolio is actually positioned, you can strip away the noise and build something that works better not just on paper, but also when the market gets volatile.

They Miss the "Why" Behind Your Allocation

Most portfolios are built around a risk score generated by a 10-question survey. But what if the risk isn't about volatility, but about missing your chance to buy a second business? What if you're willing to accept some drawdown in exchange for higher income, or trade short-term stability for long-term growth?

We believe portfolios should be built around what matters most to you. That could mean using a narrow Roth conversion window to save hundreds of thousands in future taxes, structuring the sale of a business so more wealth stays in your family, or creating a legacy plan that passes assets to the next generation tax-free. It might be funding a dream property, stepping into the next chapter of your career on your terms, or ensuring a parent's care without financial strain.

Whatever the priority, the portfolio should be shaped around it — not around a score from a questionnaire.

2:
The Three Goals of a Real Portfolio

Clarity, income, and growth – all built around your real life, so your portfolio works for you in every season.

Once you understand why most portfolios fail to perform, the next step is to define what success actually looks like. A real portfolio – one that reflects your goals, your income, and your tax situation – should be built with three primary objectives:

1. **Preserve and grow wealth**
2. **Generate reliable, increasing income**
3. **Enhance after-tax returns through strategy and timing**

These aren't theoretical. They're the same goals most of our clients express – whether they're business owners planning a liquidity event, professionals in their peak earning years, or families thinking about generational wealth.

1. Preserve and Grow Wealth

Wealth preservation isn't about avoiding risk. It's about taking the right risks for your stage of life and your broader financial picture. Know where your volatility already lives, whether in real estate, a private business, or a concentrated stock position, and design your liquid portfolio to offset it and strengthen your overall position.

Growth, on the other hand, needs to be intentional. If you're still earning, you may not need to generate income from your portfolio. That means you can lean more aggressively into growth strategies, as long as they're appropriately tax-managed. Even if you're post-liquidity or in early retirement, you may need growth just to outpace inflation and meet rising lifestyle expenses.

In both cases, growing your capital isn't about gambling. It's about owning the right mix of equity, real estate, and thematic assets that align with your personal situation and needs.

2. Generate Reliable, Increasing Income

Income doesn't just mean bonds. For most of our clients, fixed income from bonds play a surprisingly small role. Income can come from preferred stocks, REITs, MLPs, dividend-paying equities, and real estate. More importantly, it needs to be structured to rise over time, not erode due to inflation.

If your real estate portfolio already provides substantial cash flow, your liquid portfolio might be more growth oriented. But if you're relying on the liquid portfolio to supplement your income, it should be built for durability. That means managing sequence risk, smoothing volatility, and ensuring that yield doesn't come at the cost of principal decay.

Also consider the taxation of income. A 6% yield might sound attractive, but if it's taxed as ordinary income, it might be far less efficient than a 4% qualified dividend. For trusts or high-income earners, managing income placement across accounts (brokerage, IRA, Roth) can make a six-figure difference over time. The higher the tax-bracket, the more important this becomes.

3. Enhance After-Tax Returns Through Strategy and Timing

Gross return is meaningless if you're losing too much to taxes. Many investors end up paying more than they should, simply because their portfolios were never built with tax efficiency in mind.

Strategic asset location (what you hold in each type of account), tax-loss harvesting, charitable giving strategies, and planned realization of capital gains can all significantly improve your after-tax outcome. For example, a $1 million portfolio generating an 8 percent return could easily produce two very different net results depending on how it's structured.

It's not about complexity for its own sake. It's about being thoughtful. You don't need 200 positions or hedge fund tactics. You just need a plan that takes your actual tax profile, withdrawal schedule, and income sources into account.

The Balancing Act Between Growth and Income

One of the biggest challenges for high-net-worth investors is deciding how to balance growth and income. Many assume they must choose one or the other. In reality, an effective portfolio blends both by strategically allocating for long-term appreciation while at the same time generating income that supports flexibility and planning.

Real Case: Designing Liquidity Without Sacrificing Growth

A client in his mid-50s who was still working and earning over $600,000 annually didn't need income today, but he did need liquidity and flexibility for future business ventures. We allocated a portion of his portfolio toward growth-oriented assets, while also building an income sleeve that would allow for opportunistic investing or tax-efficient gifting to family members.

Your Stage of Life Shapes Your Priorities

The balance between growth, income, and tax efficiency shifts as life changes. At 45, a high-earning entrepreneur may focus on growth and tax strategies to keep liabilities low and wealth compounding. By 60, with retirement on the horizon, the focus often moves toward income stability, capital preservation, and liquidity. Even within the same age group, priorities can look very different depending on career stage, family needs, and the makeup of outside assets.

That's why cookie-cutter models often miss the mark. Most portfolios built from standardized risk tolerance questionnaires assign you to a model based on how you feel about short-term volatility, but they rarely account for things like upcoming liquidity needs, the timing of major asset sales, or windows of opportunity for tax planning. These are variables that should never be ignored and often drive real outcomes.

Scenario-based modeling shows you the ripple effects of your decisions before you make them. Say you shift a portion of your portfolio from growth-oriented equities into a tax-deferred vehicle. On paper, you're lowering this year's taxable income. But in practice, you might be stacking future withdrawals that push you into a higher bracket, impact Social Security taxation, or trigger higher Medicare premiums. Sometimes solving one problem quietly creates another, which is why you need the full picture to make the right call.

On the flip side, reducing tax-deferred balances early through Roth conversions might create a short-term tax liability but lead to long-term flexibility. With more tax-free growth and fewer future RMDs, the portfolio becomes more adaptable to a range of retirement and estate planning scenarios.

These decisions aren't simply about returns. They require understanding how income, timing, and taxes interact across multiple accounts. A portfolio must be viewed in context and coordinated across all account types and designed around real-life transitions.

The best portfolio strategies emerge from deeper conversations. Instead of asking, "What's your risk tolerance?" a better approach is to ask, "What's on the horizon? Are there any major life changes coming up? How flexible do you need your income to be in the next five years?" These questions uncover far more than a generic asset mix ever could.

As personal goals shift, your investment strategy should shift with them. A thoughtful approach blends performance with flexibility and keeps you ahead of change, not reacting to it after the fact.

Compounding Tax Alpha Over Time

Tax efficiency isn't just about reducing this year's bill. It's about maximizing compounding over decades. A 1% difference in after-tax return on a $2 million portfolio could mean over $700,000 more in wealth after 20 years. And that difference often comes not from picking better stocks, but from smarter account structure, withdrawal order, and income management.

The focus shouldn't always be about "beating the market," which is never guaranteed no matter how good the investment portfolio is. Beating inefficiency is one of the few guaranteed ways to boost returns. Every dollar saved on avoidable taxes, every missed opportunity captured, every portfolio realigned to match actual goals is money that goes straight to the bottom line. That's how real wealth compounds: by eliminating the silent drags that hold it back.

Your portfolio should reflect your purpose, not just your profile.

The rest of this book will explore how to build portfolios that accomplish all three goals: through real-world design, not theoretical allocation. Because if your portfolio isn't preserving, growing, and optimizing your wealth, then what exactly is it doing?

3:
Income-Driven Allocation in a Low-Yield World

This isn't about going back to old-school, bond-heavy investing. It's about redefining income so it works in today's markets, keeping it reliable, tax-efficient, and built to grow with you.

For most high-income investors, the idea of building a portfolio around income seems outdated. That's mostly true – traditional bond-heavy strategies fall short in today's interest rate environment. But income, when constructed intentionally, remains one of the most powerful components of a resilient portfolio.

What's changed is how we source it.

The New Income Toolkit

Gone are the days when government bonds and CDs could reliably support a retirement or supplement cash flow. Today's income-oriented portfolio needs to pull from a wider range of tools:

- Preferred stocks offer higher yields than common equity with a more stable payment profile.
- REITs provide access to real estate cash flow without direct ownership responsibilities.
- MLPs (master limited partnerships) give exposure to infrastructure and energy assets with attractive distributions.
- Dividend-growth equities combine income with long-term capital appreciation.

The point is not to chase yield for its own sake. The point is to construct an income engine that's dependable, tax-efficient, and inflation-adjusted.

Bonds Still Have a Role – Just a Smarter One

Fixed income is not dead. It just needs to be used more surgically. For clients with short-term liquidity needs, we'll often carve out a portion of the portfolio into high-quality municipals, short-duration credit, or TIPS.

But for those with flexibility, we might prefer to take some risk with higher-yielding equity income positions while keeping a cash buffer for optionality. The traditional laddered bond portfolio just doesn't make sense when inflation and rates are volatile and capital efficiency matters.

Yield is Not Yield if It's Tax-Inefficient

One of the most overlooked aspects of income investing is the tax treatment of the yield itself. A 5.5% corporate bond in a taxable account may yield less after tax than a 4% municipal bond. A REIT dividend may be taxed as ordinary income, while a qualified dividend from a dividend stock can be taxed more favorably.

A thoughtful income portfolio doesn't just seek the highest yield – it seeks the most sustainable, tax-efficient income possible. That's why we often build income portfolios differently depending on the account type (more on that in Chapter 6).

When to Trade Liquidity for Yield

This is one of the most strategic decisions a portfolio manager can make: when to give up instant liquidity in exchange for better income and return potential. The answer depends on the investor.

If a client already has a cash-flowing real estate portfolio and no near-term capital needs, allocating 10 to 15 percent of their portfolio to less liquid, long-duration strategies such as infrastructure debt, private real estate funds, or timberland can make sense. On the other hand, if liquidity is essential, we would lean more toward highly liquid income options like short-term bonds, dividend-focused ETFs, or money market funds, even if the yield is lower.

There's no single answer. But the decision should always be made with context.

Building an Income Stream That Scales With You

Income portfolios should not just meet current needs, they should adapt and grow. A well-designed income strategy can scale over time, especially for investors transitioning from active earnings to greater reliance on portfolio income.

We often structure income portfolios in layers:
- The first layer might include core dividend payers for predictable cash flow.
- The second layer includes growth-oriented income sources like dividend growth stocks or real estate.
- A third layer might include selectively illiquid strategies like private funds or real assets that enhance long-term return without daily liquidity.

By thinking in terms of layers, investors can align yield, risk, and liquidity with their personal timeline and avoid selling core holdings in a down market.

The Psychology of Income

One overlooked benefit of an income-oriented portfolio is psychological. During market downturns, clients with strong income streams often feel less pressure to panic or "do something." Knowing that their portfolio is still generating income gives them the confidence to stay invested and ride out volatility.

During the COVID-19 sell-off, several of our income-focused clients didn't flinch. Their monthly income still arrived, allowing them to maintain lifestyle and even had the opportunity to reinvest unused income to buy more into their positions at lower prices.

Income not only funds lifestyle, it supports better decision-making.

Real Case: Upgrading Yield Without Sacrificing Safety

A 62-year-old client had retired early and was partially living off his portfolio. Rising inflation was a concern. His holdings leaned heavily on intermediate-term bonds and dividend ETFs with limited upside.

We preserved his stability but replaced underperforming bond funds with:

- Actively managed REIT strategies with inflation hedging.
- High-quality preferred shares with call protection.
- A tactical sleeve of dividend-growth equities.

The outcome was higher after-tax income, better inflation protection, and no increase in portfolio volatility.

Income is not old-fashioned. It's foundational. And when constructed with purpose, it becomes the engine that keeps your strategy moving forward, regardless of what the market does.

4: Thematic Investing with an Edge

Trends become fortunes for those ready to act, not those waiting for certainty.

Markets don't just move in cycles. They move in waves of innovation, policy shifts, and global transformation. A static portfolio built on yesterday's economy is unlikely to succeed in tomorrow's world. That's where thematic investing comes in.

Thematic investing is about putting part of your portfolio behind the forces that actually move markets. It's not gambling on headlines. It's identifying long-term shifts that reshape industries and channel capital, then positioning early enough to benefit as they play out.

Investing in Real-World Trends

The best themes to invest in aren't trends that flare up and fade away. They're durable forces with real economic weight, driven by legislation, public investment, and necessity. These aren't passing narratives. They're structural shifts that will define markets for decades.

Consider:
- **Energy transition**: Hydrogen, nuclear, and grid storage.
- **Defense and geopolitics**: Reshoring of critical industries, cybersecurity, and advanced defense technology.
- **Infrastructure modernization**: Water treatment, broadband expansion, electrical grid upgrades, and smart transit systems.
- **Artificial intelligence and automation**: The digitization of labor, robotics, and productivity transformation across all industries.

- **Demographic shifts**: Aging populations, increased healthcare demand, and the rise of a global middle class with new consumption patterns.

Thematic investing allows investors to benefit from how the world is changing, not from guessing what the next quarterly earnings report will be.

But finding the right entry point matters. Investing early in a new trend can be highly rewarding. Investing late can be costly. That's why due diligence, sizing, and understanding the maturity of a theme are critical.

The Hydrogen Revolution and Asymmetric Bets

Take hydrogen as an example. Hydrogen has the potential to reshape industrial processes, shipping, and long-haul transport. It's not just a technology headline. It's a policy-backed, infrastructure-heavy solution attracting serious attention from governments and corporations worldwide.

Dozens of nations have passed hydrogen roadmaps. The U.S. Department of Energy is funding regional hydrogen hubs. Automotive, aerospace, and industrial giants across the world are investing directly into hydrogen technologies.

This creates fertile ground for early-stage companies to gain market share. But these opportunities come with real risk: technology risk, policy risk, and funding risk.

That's why we treat these investments as **asymmetric bets**. These are positions where the potential upside significantly outweighs the downside. If you invest 2 percent of your portfolio into a hydrogen company and it grows tenfold, that one decision could materially improve your long-term returns. If the company fails, the impact on your total portfolio is minimal.

We don't recommend large positions in speculative themes. But a total portfolio allocation of 3 to 5 percent across a few asymmetric ideas can keep the portfolio forward-looking without compromising stability.

How to Size and Manage Thematic Positions

Thematic investing should never replace your core portfolio. It should complement it. We typically structure portfolios in layers, each serving a specific purpose:

- **Core**: Broad market exposure that captures long-term equity growth.
- **Income**: Reliable, tax-efficient cash flow sources that fund flexibility.
- **Tactical**: Dynamic positions based on short- to mid-term themes and market dislocations.
- **Asymmetric**: High-conviction, high-potential ideas with a small position size and defined exit strategy.

Thematic investments often fit in the tactical or asymmetric layer. Your conviction and timeline determine the allocation. For example, a theme like infrastructure modernization, which is supported by bipartisan funding, may justify a larger position than an early-stage biotech play.

Risk management is not just about size. It also includes:

- **Exit planning:** Knowing your criteria for trimming or exiting.
- **Diversification within themes:** Avoiding overconcentration in a single company or fund.
- **Monitoring policy shifts:** Tracking regulation and subsidy changes that may impact your thesis.

Aligning Capital With Conviction

Thematic investing also allows investors to align their portfolios with their values. A client interested in clean energy doesn't just want to earn a return. They want to be part of something that matters. That personal connection can strengthen discipline, especially during market volatility.

It's easy to hold a position when you believe in the reason behind it, even during extreme or heavy ups and downs. Conviction gives you the discipline to stay invested when others panic, and the clarity to act when real opportunities show up.

This is where real portfolio design becomes personal. Themes don't just provide diversification. They provide meaning. They help investors stay engaged, informed, and optimistic about the future.

Designing Portfolios That Do a Job

At BFG Wealth Management, we don't believe in one-size-fits-all model portfolios. We build strategy frameworks – Core, Income, Tactical, and Asymmetric – that serve different financial purposes and reflect our clients' real lives. These framework templates help clients think critically about why each asset exists, not just where it lives.

Core Growth

A foundation of broad equity exposure intended for long-term compounding. Core portfolios may include:
- Broad U.S. and global equity ETFs or funds.
- Market-cap-based diversification.
- Tax-aware positioning to limit turnover in taxable accounts.

This provides durable upside without high maintenance.

Income and Stability
A portfolio layer focused on reliable cash flow and risk resilience. We might include:

- REITs and dividend payers.
- High-quality fixed income (municipals, short-term corporate, inflation-linked, money market).
- Private funds when appropriate.

This layer adds liquidity and stability, acting as a buffer during volatility. It gives us the flexibility to cover expenses, rebalance when opportunities arise, and reduce the need to sell long-term holdings during market stress.

Tactical and Thematic Tilt
These are overweight exposures aligned with significant economic or technological shifts, such as:

- Energy transition (hydrogen, grid storage).
- Innovation in technology (AI, robotics).
- Defense, infrastructure modernization, or demographic trends.

All thematic bets are tactically sized at typically 1–3 percent per theme to improve return potential while limiting risk.

Asymmetric Opportunity
This layer captures early-stage or speculative ideas – small positions with high potential upside.

They might include:

- Early-stage micro-caps.
- Niche innovation vehicles.

- Special situations where the risk is limited but the potential reward is significant.

Each of these positions is sized to a level where upside is meaningful but downside is contained.

5:

Real Estate as a Portfolio Engine

When your real estate and investment portfolios work together, every dollar you own starts pulling in the same direction.

Real estate is often treated as separate from "the portfolio," but for many investors it's a core financial driver. It can deliver income, equity growth, tax benefits, and flexibility that few other asset classes can offer.

The challenge isn't whether real estate belongs in your investment strategy. It's how to integrate it effectively.

Direct Ownership vs. REITs vs. DSTs

There are multiple ways to gain exposure to real estate. Each comes with tradeoffs:

- **Direct ownership** offers the most control, tax shelter, and upside potential. It also requires time, management, and liquidity planning.
- **REITs** (Real Estate Investment Trusts) provide diversification and liquidity with little involvement. However, they tend to have more market correlation and tax complexity.
- **DSTs** (Delaware Statutory Trusts) allow 1031 exchange investors to roll into institutional-grade real estate passively. This is especially useful for aging landlords or owners looking to retire without taking a tax hit.

The right approach depends on your stage of life, tax bracket, time commitment, and cash flow needs. Often, a hybrid model works best.

We work with many clients who maintain around three to five rental properties for income and appreciation, while also holding REITs in retirement accounts for liquidity and diversification.

Others have exited direct ownership entirely and transitioned into DSTs to eliminate landlord responsibilities while maintaining 1031 exchange eligibility. A 1031 exchange allows investors to defer capital gains taxes by reinvesting the proceeds from one property into another like-kind property. Instead of selling and paying a large tax bill upfront, you keep more capital working for you while repositioning into assets that fit your stage of life. It is one of the most effective tools for compounding wealth inside real estate.

There is no universal answer, but there is always a strategic one.

The BRRR Strategy: More Than Just a Tactic

BRRR (Buy, Rehab, Rent, Refinance, Repeat) is a way to scale real estate exposure by recycling capital. It turns equity into a tool instead of a static value. If done right, it allows investors to keep growing without constant new capital contributions.

It's not for everyone. BRRR requires planning, risk tolerance, and access to capital. But for those already familiar with real estate, it's a strategy that can deliver strong returns with tax-deferred compounding.

Real Case: From Two to Fifteen Properties With BRRR

One of our clients, an entrepreneur in his early 40s, used the BRRR method to grow his portfolio from two to fifteen rental homes in under five years. This was all while maintaining a full-time business and a young family. By strategically refinancing after each rehab, he recaptured capital, reinvested it, and built a snowball effect that created both cash flow and equity growth.

During this time, he also continued to steadily grow his liquid investment portfolio, ensuring that he had a diversified base outside of real estate. Some of the profits from his investment account were strategically pulled to help fund new property acquisitions, allowing him to scale his rental holdings without overleveraging or depleting cash reserves. This balance between liquid and illiquid assets gave him both the long-term appreciation potential of real estate and the flexibility of accessible capital.

In portfolio planning, we often treat BRRR properties as a blend of equity growth and cash flow. Much like a high-yield stock with optionality. The goal is to recognize it for what it is. A real component of your investment engine, not an outside asset.

Real Estate as a Bond Proxy with Upside

In today's environment, rental real estate can be seen as a fixed-income alternative. Cap rates of 6 to 9 percent in some markets mean your yield can exceed many bond portfolios. Add in depreciation, appreciation, and refinancing potential, and you have an asset that may offer more stability and upside than traditional income sources.

For example, a $400,000 property rented at $2,800 per month might yield a net cash return of 7 percent annually after expenses. This is before factoring in principal paydown and property appreciation. On top of that, depreciation may shield most of that income from current taxation, improving after-tax yield substantially.

Another powerful feature of rental real estate is its ability to provide inflation-adjusted income. Unlike most fixed-income securities where interest payments are static, rental rates can be adjusted over time to keep pace with or even outpace inflation. This means that as the cost of living rises, your rental income can rise as well, helping to preserve the real purchasing power of that income stream. This dynamic makes real estate a valuable hedge against the erosive effects of inflation, especially in long-term retirement income planning.

This doesn't mean real estate is risk-free. Tenants, maintenance, vacancies, and property-specific issues all exist. But in a well-diversified plan, real estate plays a stabilizing role that deserves thoughtful integration.

Integrating Real Estate into the Portfolio

This is where most advisors fall short. They either ignore real estate completely or treat it as a separate conversation. We take a different approach.

We model rental income alongside investment income. We stress test property equity under rising rates or declining rents. We assess whether existing holdings are functioning as yield, growth, or tax tools. Then we evaluate how that shifts the mix in the broader portfolio.

This matters especially when it comes to:

- Adjusting public equity exposure to account for concentrated real estate positions.
- Planning liquidity for property upgrades, taxes, or future 1031 exchanges.
- Replacing income needs with passive cash flow from rentals or DSTs.
- Choosing whether to hold properties in trusts, LLCs, or directly for estate planning.

Different types of real estate behave differently too, and a well-structured portfolio accounts for those distinctions. Residential rentals can provide more consistent monthly income but may carry higher management demands. Commercial properties can offer longer leases and potentially higher yields, but they are often more sensitive to economic cycles. Agricultural or farm properties may deliver stable returns and unique tax advantages, but their performance can hinge on commodity prices and weather patterns. By understanding the risk and return profiles of each asset class, investors can better position real estate to complement rather than conflict with the rest of their holdings.

When clients have both meaningful liquid assets and established property investments, real estate becomes a core financial pillar rather than an add-on. Treating it as part of the broader strategy ensures the portfolio is fully aligned, tax-optimized, and resilient across market cycles.

6:
Portfolio Design by Account Type

When each dollar is in the right place, taxes shrink, flexibility grows, and your plan gets stronger without adding risk.

Most portfolios are discussed in terms of holdings – stocks, bonds, funds – but rarely by where those holdings live. Yet the account type you use to own an investment can be just as important as the investment itself. Asset selection determines what you earn. Asset location determines what you keep.

High-net-worth investors often have their wealth spread across taxable brokerage accounts, IRAs, Roth IRAs, and trusts. Each comes with its own tax rules, distribution requirements, and strategic opportunities. Understanding how to spread assets across these different account types is one of the most powerful ways to improve after-tax returns – and it's often ignored.

Taxable vs. Tax-Deferred vs. Tax-Free
Let's start with the basics:

Taxable accounts (Individual, Joint, or Trust): These are the most flexible accounts. You can access your money at any time, but you'll pay capital gains taxes on profits and annual taxes on dividends and interest.

Tax-deferred accounts (Traditional IRA, SEP IRA, 401(k), 403(b)): Investments grow without taxes until withdrawn. But distributions are taxed as ordinary income, which can create large tax liabilities in retirement if not planned for.

Tax-free accounts (Roth IRA, Roth 401(k)): These are funded with after-tax dollars, but all qualified withdrawals, including gains, are completely tax-free. Roth accounts are especially valuable because they allow for strategic tax-free compounding.

The Type of Income Matters
Each investment produces a different kind of income: qualified dividends, ordinary interest, capital gains, or tax-advantaged distributions. The type of income should influence where you place it. For example:

- Hold REITs or high-yield bonds in IRAs, where the ordinary income they produce won't trigger an annual tax bill.
- Keep growth stocks in taxable accounts to take advantage of long-term capital gains rates and tax-loss harvesting; or
- Use Roth IRAs for small-cap or asymmetric investments that could grow significantly, because any gains come out tax-free.

This is known as **asset location** – placing the right investments in the right accounts to minimize taxes and maximize long-term growth.

Asset Location Strategy in Practice
Here's a simple framework to start with:

Taxable Accounts:
- Municipal bonds (tax-exempt).
- ETFs and index funds with low turnover.
- Long-term growth stocks.
- Separately managed accounts using tax-loss harvesting.

Traditional IRA or 401(k):
- REITs and MLPs that generate ordinary income.
- High-yield bonds.

- Actively managed funds or strategies that would create short-term gains if held in taxable accounts

Roth IRA or Roth 401(k):
- High-growth equities.
- Small-cap stocks.
- Alternative assets or private investments with high upside potential.

While this structure won't show up in your quarterly performance report, it will show up in your long-term results through reduced taxes, more flexible withdrawals, and better control over your retirement income.

Withdrawal Planning and the Long Game
Asset location also sets you up for smarter withdrawal strategies later in life.

For example:
- During early retirement, you might draw from taxable accounts first, allowing tax-deferred accounts to continue growing.
- In low-income years, you might convert IRA assets to Roth, filling up lower tax brackets and avoiding higher Required Minimum Distributions (RMDs) later.
- Having assets in a Roth can give you the option to make tax-free withdrawals in years where other income is unusually high, such as from a business sale or property liquidation.

This isn't just theory. It's one of the ways real tax alpha shows up, not just in any one year, but across a lifetime.

Real Case: Turning Misplaced Assets Into Tax Efficiency

A client came to us with $2.4 million spread across three accounts: $1.2 million in a taxable brokerage, $900,000 in a Traditional IRA, and $300,000 in a Roth IRA. Their previous advisor had given each account the same asset mix: a 60/40 blend of stocks and bonds.

That meant their Roth IRA, arguably their most powerful account, was holding 40 percent bonds, including municipal bonds. This is one of the most common mistakes we see.

Municipal bonds are tax-advantaged for taxable accounts. Placing them in a Roth IRA, which is already tax-free, wastes their benefit. Worse, holding bonds in Roth space meant less room for growth-oriented investments, which defeats the purpose of the Roth in the first place.

We redesigned the structure:
- **IRA:** High-yield income assets, REITs, and bond funds with regular income.
- **Taxable:** Long-term equities with a focus on tax-loss harvesting and low turnover..
- **Roth IRA:** Small-cap growth stocks and asymmetric themes with high potential upside

The result? No increase in overall risk, but a higher expected after-tax return. The Roth account was positioned to compound faster. The IRA was now generating reliable income without triggering current tax. The taxable account had a clear loss harvesting plan. Same dollars, better design.

Blending Account Strategy with Investment Strategy
Too often, advisors build portfolios without thinking about account type. They focus only on "what to buy" without thinking about

"where to hold it." But when we blend account strategy with investment strategy, we get:

- Better tax outcomes.
- Greater control over retirement income.
- More flexibility for gifts, trust funding, and legacy planning.
- Less surprise when it's time to sell or during market corrections.

Tax efficiency isn't about avoiding taxes altogether. It's about minimizing friction by using the rules that already exist to your advantage.

Designing by account type doesn't replace your investment strategy. It amplifies it. Just like you wouldn't build a house without considering the foundation, you shouldn't build a portfolio without thinking about account structure.

If your current advisor isn't asking where each asset is held and why, you might not be getting the most from your wealth.

7:

Risk Management Without Killing Return

Risk is inevitable – damage is optional. Build in protection now, so when markets turn, you're ready to act instead of react.

If you're investing for real wealth, not just retirement, you can't afford to ignore risk. But you also can't afford to eliminate it entirely. The real goal of risk management isn't to avoid volatility, it's to avoid ruin. There's a big difference.

Volatility Is Not the Enemy

Too many investors confuse volatility with loss. Volatility is just movement. It's part of how markets behave. And for long-term investors, it's often necessary to produce outsized gains. The problem comes when volatility is paired with forced selling, because that's when temporary losses become permanent ones.

We help clients manage volatility by building in buffers. That might mean:

- Keeping 6 to 12 months of cash or short-term liquidity.
- Aligning risk exposure with actual timelines for using capital.
- Using income-generating investments to smooth return profiles.

When you're not forced to sell in a downturn, volatility becomes survivable, and even useful. Being able to ride through the dips without panicking allows investors to capture the eventual recovery and maintain their compounding momentum.

Volatility can even present opportunity. For long-term investors with dry powder, meaning cash or liquid investments ready to deploy, downturns can be the moment to pick up quality assets at lower prices. But that's only true if the core portfolio is built to withstand the ride.

Position Sizing and Risk Concentration

No matter how good an investment looks, it should never threaten your portfolio. That's why we cap high-risk or speculative positions at small percentages. A 3 percent position that goes to zero won't derail your plan. But a 20 percent position that drops 70 percent can set you back years.

Position sizing is one of the simplest and most effective tools for risk management. It's not just about limiting the downside; it's about how you give your winners room to run without letting them dominate your allocation. We've seen clients hold on to winning stocks or sectors far too long, only to watch their portfolio concentration silently build. When the correction comes, it hits harder than expected.

Smart position sizing also helps with decision clarity. Knowing that a speculative holding represents just 2 percent of your portfolio allows you to make cleaner, more rational decisions without emotion dominating your response. It gives you space to say, "this could go to zero, and that's okay."

This is particularly relevant with thematic investments, such as emerging technologies or alternative assets. Asymmetric opportunities, those with limited downside and large potential upside, can be powerful but only when sized correctly. The goal is to participate in the upside without betting the house.

Tactical Risk Adjustments

We don't believe in trying to time the market. But we do believe in being responsive. That means occasionally trimming exposure when markets are euphoric or adding selectively when they're fearful.

This is not about calling tops and bottoms. It's about managing risk exposures in real time. For example, when valuations become historically stretched and sentiment is frothy, we may reduce equity exposure slightly or rotate into sectors with more reasonable pricing. On the flip side, when fear dominates and quality assets are on sale, we look to add selectively.

Tactical risk management doesn't mean swinging your allocation wildly. It means making informed, measured adjustments that reflect real-world risks and opportunities. Think of it like steering, not slamming your brakes.

This type of flexibility is especially useful during periods of regime change: when inflation, interest rates, or geopolitical tensions create sustained market shifts. Having the ability to tactically shift between asset classes, sectors, or geographies gives the portfolio room to adapt without abandoning its long-term strategy.

Staying Invested Without Being Exposed

The biggest long-term risk is not short-term volatility, it's missing out on long-term compounding. The cost of sitting in cash for too long is often greater than the drawdown risk of being invested wisely.

Of course, that doesn't mean ignoring risk altogether. Instead, we design portfolios with built-in resilience:

- **Diversified income sources** to weather market shifts and provide steady cash flow.
- **Allocation sleeves** that respond to different economic conditions (e.g., inflation hedges, defensive sectors).

- **Liquidity layers** that give clients confidence during downturns and prevent forced selling.

The key is to structure portfolios so they can absorb market turbulence without requiring drastic action. That might mean:

- Holding a mix of public and private assets to balance liquidity and return potential.
- Including floating-rate or inflation-linked securities to hedge against unexpected rate moves.
- Using targeted allocations to metals and broad commodities in small doses to help offset equity market volatility and preserve purchasing power during inflationary periods.

For many investors, the real value lies in having options – ways to respond to changing conditions without having to liquidate core holdings.

Behavioral Risk is Real Risk

It's not just market movements that destroy wealth; it's how investors react to them. Behavioral risk is one of the biggest threats to long-term success. Panic selling at the bottom. Chasing performance at the top. Over-trading. Under-reacting. These behaviors often cost more than the market downturn itself.

In today's environment, this risk is amplified because retail investors now play a much larger role in the markets than they did just five years ago. The rise of commission-free trading, investment apps, and social media has created waves of participation that can drive volatility and sentiment. What used to be primarily institutional flows now includes millions of individual decisions that often move markets in real time. For long-term investors, this means more noise, sharper swings, and an even greater need for discipline.

That's why our approach to risk management always includes a behavioral component:

- We walk through stress tests and downside scenarios so clients understand what to expect.
- We build in liquidity so there's no need to sell at the worst time.
- We use layered portfolios that separate growth, income, and cash so each part has a role and a purpose.
- We set a clearly defined 5-year price target for each position, creating a long-term reference point that helps clients look past short-term volatility and stay disciplined.

This kind of structure doesn't just protect against loss – it protects against fear. When fear is off the table, clients can stay committed to the plan.

Real Case: Rebalancing Wealth for Stability and Peace of Mind

One client came to us with a $5 million portfolio heavily concentrated in tech stocks. They'd seen incredible returns over the last decade but knew the exposure was becoming dangerous. After reviewing their liquidity needs and risk tolerance, we gradually trimmed their top holdings and rotated into other sectors, building a more balanced core. We also carved out a cash reserve so they wouldn't feel pressured to sell during the next correction.

Another client held multiple rental properties but was extremely cash-light. Their net worth looked great on paper, but any drop in rental income or property values would have created pressure to sell. We helped them refinance into longer-term debt, improve their cash buffer, and diversify some proceeds into liquid income investments. That gave them breathing room, and peace of mind.

In both cases, risk wasn't eliminated. It was acknowledged, rebalanced, and planned for.

Optionality Is a Form of Protection

One of the more advanced ways to think about risk is through the lens of optionality. When your portfolio is flexible, when you have liquidity, and when you have non-correlated assets, you have more options. More options mean better decisions, and fewer forced ones.

Optionality might look like:
- Keeping some capital in liquid, low-volatility strategies that can be deployed opportunistically.
- Holding assets in a Roth IRA for tax-free withdrawals during high-income years.
- Having direct ownership in real estate or other private funds that are not tied to the stock market's daily swings.

This kind of flexibility doesn't always show up in performance reports, but it shows up in outcomes. In lower stress. In fewer mistakes. In higher resilience.

The Goal is Not Zero Risk. The Goal is Durable Wealth.

Every investor faces risk. It's an inescapable part of participating in any financial market. The real question isn't whether risk exists, but whether your portfolio is built to withstand it. A strong design can absorb short-term shocks without forcing you into long-term mistakes.

The portfolios we design are not built to eliminate risk entirely, because that would mean eliminating return potential as well. Instead, they are structured to absorb risk intelligently. This means understanding which risks are worth taking, which can be mitigated, and which should be avoided altogether. It means providing stability without sacrificing the upside that fuels long-term growth. Most importantly, it means giving you the confidence to stay the course when it matters most.

This kind of confidence doesn't come from guesswork or blind optimism. It comes from structure. It comes from knowing that your portfolio includes multiple layers of protection: liquidity to handle unexpected needs, diversification to spread exposure, and allocation strategies that align with your income and tax planning. It comes from knowing you've considered the "what if" scenarios and that your wealth is positioned to handle them.

Real wealth isn't built by avoiding all risk. It's built by managing the right risks in the right proportions, with a clear plan and the flexibility to adapt over time. That includes market risk, but also inflation risk, interest rate risk, sequence of returns risk, tax policy risk, and liquidity risk. A well-designed portfolio is aware of all of these, not paralyzed by them.

For example, if all your assets are tied up in long-term growth positions with no near-term liquidity, even a temporary downturn can force a sale at the wrong time. But if you've built in a cash reserve and layered your income generation, you gain the freedom to wait for recovery, rather than locking in a loss. That's how intelligent risk management works. It buys you time. It protects your behavior. It supports better outcomes.

If your current strategy feels fragile, overly complex, or emotionally reactive, it's probably not working hard enough for you. Cracks in the plan often stay hidden until pressure hits. When markets fall, interest rates spike, or life throws a curveball, that is the absolute worst time to find out your allocation is stretched, your liquidity is thin, or your withdrawal plan doesn't exist.

The time to fix that isn't in the middle of a crisis. It's now. When the sun is shining and there's room to make thoughtful changes, you can rework your strategy with clarity instead of urgency. You can install guardrails before the sharp turns come.

Risk is inevitable. But damage is not. The difference lies in the design.

8:
Your Portfolio Is Not a Pie Chart

Your life isn't built in neat slices. Your portfolio shouldn't be either. Layer it so every dollar has a job, every asset serves a purpose, and every part works together.

Traditional investment presentations love pie charts. They make everything look clean, organized, and proportionally balanced. But real portfolios aren't built in slices. They're built in layers, with different components serving different purposes depending on your goals, timeline, and total financial picture.

The classic pie chart masks this complexity. It gives the illusion of diversification without showing how the pieces actually work together and unfortunately sometimes, against each other.

Think in Layers, Not Slices

Instead of trying to fit everything into one graphic, we structure portfolios in functional layers:

- **Core**: This is your foundation. Often broad equity exposure, high-quality fixed income, or ETFs that anchor the strategy and provide long-term growth with moderate volatility.

- **Income**: These are assets specifically selected to generate reliable cash flow-REITs, preferreds, dividend-paying stocks, and rental real estate.

- **Tactical**: This layer responds to economic trends and current market positioning. It includes timely overweighting to sectors like energy, infrastructure, defense, or healthcare depending on macro developments.

- **Asymmetric**: High-conviction, high-upside ideas that are small in size but potentially meaningful-like thematic tech, early-stage hydrogen, micro-cap equities, or special situations.

Layering allows us to balance long-term growth with short-term flexibility. It also enables better alignment with a client's total life structure, including business interests, future liquidity events, and tax considerations.

Most importantly, the layered approach gives each part of the portfolio a role. That leads to better decisions. Instead of asking, "Is this asset class good or bad?" we ask, "What job is this asset doing in the portfolio?"

Integrating Real Estate, Business Equity, and Inheritance
Many of our clients hold significant assets outside their brokerage account: real estate, business ownership, or planned inheritance. These holdings often carry more risk, more leverage, or more concentration than a traditional mutual fund portfolio.

If we ignore these assets, we create duplication or blind spots. If we integrate them, we can design the rest of the portfolio to complement them.

This means:
- Offsetting concentrated business risk with broader diversification elsewhere.
- Managing liquidity around real estate holding periods or capital events.
- Preparing investment allocations around potential estate transfer timelines.

- Including cash flow forecasts that reflect passive income streams.

We call this a **global balance sheet** approach. It looks at every asset, liability, and cash flow together so nothing is managed in isolation. The full picture leads to better allocation, smarter risk management, and a portfolio aligned with your entire financial life.

For example, if a client owns multiple short-term rentals that generate $200,000 a year in income, it would make little sense to focus their investment account on dividend payers. We may instead target long-term growth, inflation protection, or tax deferral. Similarly, if a business makes up 80 percent of a client's net worth, our goal is to ensure the remaining 20 percent is extremely flexible, liquid, and diversified.

When you ignore these broader holdings, you're designing a portfolio for 20 percent of the client's life-and hoping it works for 100 percent of their goals.

The Family Office Mindset-Without Needing $100M

You don't need to be ultra-wealthy to benefit from Family Office thinking. The core idea is simple: bring structure and strategy to the entire financial ecosystem, not just the investable assets.

That includes:
- Coordinating with your CPA or estate attorney.
- Planning around charitable goals or legacy considerations.
- Managing cash flow across taxable and tax-deferred vehicles.
- Stress testing for events like a business sale, major purchase, or life transition.
- Centralizing decision-making across trusts, entities, and real estate holdings.

Family Offices are known for their comprehensive integration. But even families with $1M to $10M and beyond can take a similar approach-with the right advisor and team.

We've helped clients build structures where:
- Real estate cash flow supports early retirement goals.
- Roth conversions are synchronized with low-income years to reduce future RMDs.
- Trust accounts are used strategically to fund next-generation education or home purchases.
- Inheritance planning includes tax modeling, asset matching, and gift planning years in advance.

When you think like a Family Office, your capital becomes more intentional. Every dollar has a role. Every asset serves a purpose. Every part of your life – legal, tax, investment, family – is speaking the same language.

What Pie Charts Don't Show

A standard pie chart might show 60 percent stocks, 30 percent bonds, and 10 percent cash. That tells you nothing about:
- What kind of stocks? U.S.? International? Growth? Value?
- What kind of bonds? Municipal? Corporate? Duration risk?
- What job does each component serve in your real life?
- What is happening outside the chart-in real estate, taxes, or income?

We've seen portfolios labeled "moderately aggressive" that included 10 bond funds and 5 equity funds, all heavily overlapping. The chart looked diversified. The portfolio was not.

True portfolio design accounts for:
- Liquidity timing: When do you need the money?

- Tax considerations: Which accounts are these assets held in?
- Risk appetite: Is your risk budget being spent where you want it?
- Opportunity alignment: Are you positioned for the next 5 years, not the last 10?

The pie chart cannot tell that story. But layered design can.

Siloed Advice Leads to Siloed Outcomes

Most financial plans and portfolios are built in isolation. The estate attorney doesn't talk to the investment advisor. The CPA doesn't know about the 1031 exchange. The client ends up playing quarterback across disconnected teams.

That's where problems start:
- Assets get duplicated in different vehicles.
- Tax strategies get overlooked.
- Liquidity mismatches occur.
- Opportunities go unrealized because no one has the full picture.

Layered portfolio design works because it assumes from day one that your life is integrated – even if your financial team isn't yet. Once your investments, taxes, estate, and cash flow are speaking the same language, the results compound.

Designing for Real Life Events

Let's say you plan to buy a building in 2 years. Should you be 100 percent in long-term equities?

Or maybe you're selling your business in 18 months. What happens to your tax bracket, and how should you position the portfolio ahead of that liquidity event?

What if your spouse inherits $2M unexpectedly? Is your existing strategy designed to integrate a sudden influx of capital with different cost basis and tax implications?

Layered design helps you adapt. You can:
- Create "future use" sleeves that are timed with known events.
- Hold cash or short-duration bonds in segments of the portfolio with upcoming liquidity needs.
- Match asset volatility to the flexibility of the dollars used.

In other words: different money has different jobs. And those jobs change over time. The goal is to ensure your portfolio reflects those realities.

Your Life Is Not a Pie Chart. Your Portfolio Shouldn't Be Either.

Good portfolios don't just balance risk and return. They balance priorities, timelines, account types, tax rules, legacy goals, and opportunity sets. A pie chart may be a fine visual, but it's not a strategy.

True portfolio design is layered, intentional, and tailored to the life you're actually living, not the one assumed by a model. If your current investment strategy still starts and ends with a pie chart, it may be time to step back and ask a deeper question:

Is my capital working in alignment with my goals, or just sitting in neatly sliced boxes?

9:
Real Investors, Real Outcomes

From scattered accounts to clear direction. From tax drag to tax efficiency. From uncertainty to confident decision-making.

These real-life examples show what happens when your money is aligned with your life.

One of the best ways to understand how real portfolio design works is to see it in action. In this chapter, we walk through anonymized client scenarios that illustrate how thoughtful planning and strategic allocation make a measurable difference. These are not case studies about beating the market. They are stories about clarity, alignment, and decisions that reduce complexity, improve tax efficiency, and give clients more control over their financial future.

From Asset Chaos to Coordinated Strategy

A business owner in his early 50s came to us with his investments spread across eight accounts at five different institutions. His investment mix included stocks, rental properties, annuities, and mutual funds, but there was no structure. No clear allocation. No coordinated plan. No understanding of how each piece fit with the others.

We began by mapping out his complete household balance sheet and cash flow model. What we found was eye-opening: overlapping investments, redundant fees, and unnecessary complexity that obscured his actual exposure and risk.

We restructured his holdings into a layered portfolio: Core, Income, Tactical, and Asymmetric. Each account was assigned a role. We consolidated redundant accounts, updated beneficiary designations, and coordinated his trust and estate documents to reflect the new architecture.

The outcome wasn't just a clearer portfolio. It was a system designed for performance, liquidity, tax efficiency, and simplicity. He went from financial noise to a strategy he could understand and act on.

Real Estate and Retirement on One Page

A couple in their mid-60s had built significant wealth through real estate. They owned four single-family rental homes and parcels of land across multiple states. But their investment accounts were still built using a cookie-cutter retirement model: mostly bonds, high-fee mutual funds, and no consideration of the real estate income they already had.

They didn't need more income. What they needed was a growth and tax strategy that would complement their rental properties. We started by integrating their rental income, depreciation schedules, and anticipated 1031 exchange plans into their financial model.

We then shifted their investable portfolio into tax-efficient growth positions. Roth IRAs were used to house asymmetric growth themes. Taxable accounts were optimized for low turnover equities. Their estate plan was updated to reflect property transfer strategies and charitable giving plans.

By looking at the total picture, not just the assets held at our custodian, we helped them reduce duplication, improve tax efficiency, and better prepare for future liquidity events.

Turning Liquidity Into Leverage

Another client came to us after selling his company for a sizeable sum. He had no plan for what to do next, other than not wanting to make any major mistakes. Most of his proceeds were in cash, and several friends had pitched private investments to him. He felt overwhelmed and stuck.

We started by segmenting his funds based on time horizon and purpose:

- 3 years of living expenses set aside in low-risk, highly liquid holdings.
- A Core portfolio to protect and grow wealth over the long term.
- A Tactical sleeve for moderate tilts based on global trends.
- An Asymmetric sleeve for limited exposure to early-stage and private deals.

We built a financial model that included charitable giving goals, future real estate purchases, and a structured Roth conversion strategy to manage long-term tax exposure.

What started as paralysis turned into purpose. Within six months, he was back to making confident decisions. Not because he knew everything, but because he finally had a framework.

A Retirement Rebuilt Around Cash Flow

One retired couple came to us concerned about running out of money. They had millions in retirement assets, but their drawdown strategy was done without any clear plan. Each year, they'd call their previous advisor and ask which account to sell from. No one was looking at taxes, investment risk, or the sequence of withdrawals.

We created a withdrawal map that blended Roth conversions, taxable account harvesting, and Social Security timing to reduce their long-term tax burden.

The portfolio itself was redesigned to:

- Use dividends and interest for predictable cash flow.

- Provide flexibility through a tactical allocation sleeve.
- Reduce RMD impact through targeted Roth conversions over five years.

With this structure, they had a 30-year income projection that was tax-optimized and stress-tested against multiple economic scenarios. Most importantly, they felt peace of mind.

Legacy Planning as Portfolio Design

A widow in her late 70s came to us with a simple request: "I want to make things easy for my kids." Her portfolio was largely in a trust, but she had multiple retirement accounts and a few individual stocks with large unrealized gains.

Rather than focusing only on performance, we focused on positioning:

- We consolidated and simplified accounts to minimize estate complexity.
- We used charitable giving tools to offset gains and align with her values.
- We optimized step-up in basis opportunities to preserve wealth for her heirs.

This was not just investment management. It was estate planning, tax strategy, and emotional clarity all working together. Her children later shared that everything was "exactly how she wanted it," and they understood the structure because it was explained to them clearly in advance.

What Working With a Real Advisor Actually Looks Like

Real investors aren't just looking for hot stock tips. They want clarity, a plan, and someone who understands the way financial decisions align with life decisions.

That's what we provide. Not a model portfolio, but a framework customized to:

- Your income sources.
- Your tax situation.
- Your timeline.
- Your goals.
- Your outside holdings.
- Your family dynamics.

Whether you're accumulating wealth, transitioning out of a business, or preparing to pass it on, your portfolio should serve a purpose-not just deliver performance. These real-life examples show what that looks like.

In each of these stories, the outcome wasn't better returns alone. It was confidence, clarity, and strategic alignment between money and life. That's what real financial advice delivers.

10:
What to Expect From a Real Advisor

The difference between managing money and managing wealth.

Most investors have worked with a financial advisor at some point in their lives. The experience can vary dramatically, ranging from a brief annual review focused on portfolio performance to a truly comprehensive planning relationship that touches every area of your financial life. The difference between those two experiences is enormous. One is transactional. The other is strategic, coordinated, and ongoing.

The role of a real advisor is not simply to pick investments or rebalance a portfolio. It's to help you design, implement, and maintain a complete financial strategy that works in the real world. That means looking at your entire financial life at once, identifying the connections between different parts of it, and making decisions that strengthen the whole picture.

A Planning-First Mindset

The investment portfolio is only one part of the equation. A true advisor begins by understanding the full context of your financial life before making a single investment recommendation.

This includes:
- Household income and expenses, including fixed obligations and discretionary spending.

- Current tax bracket and expected future tax liability based on career changes, business sales, retirement income, or inheritances.

- Business interests, real estate holdings, and any trust or estate structures already in place.

- Retirement income planning and an honest assessment of risk capacity, both financially and emotionally.

Once this broader framework is clear, the portfolio can be constructed to serve the plan. The sequence matters. Building a portfolio without this level of clarity is like building a house without a blueprint.

Communication That Is Ongoing and Proactive

Too many investors only hear from their advisor when it is time to sign paperwork or attend an annual review. A real advisor is in touch regularly, with conversations that are timely, relevant, and purposeful.

That means:
- Providing quarterly updates that explain not only how the portfolio has performed but why it is positioned the way it is.

- Scheduling strategy calls when there are significant market shifts or economic developments that could affect your plan.

- Reaching out proactively before major life events such as selling a property, receiving a windfall, or changing jobs so that tax and investment strategies can be adjusted in advance.

- Offering transparent reporting and a clear fee structure so you know exactly what you are paying for and what you are getting in return.

When markets are volatile or economic headlines are unsettling, you should already know your advisor's plan for navigating them. Silence in those moments is a warning sign.

Coordination With Your Financial Team

Your taxes, investments, and estate planning are not separate topics. They are interconnected parts of the same strategy. A skilled advisor does not operate in isolation. They coordinate with your CPA, your estate attorney, and other professionals to make sure each decision supports the others.

Examples of coordinated work include:
- Reviewing capital gains and losses before year-end to optimize your tax position.

- Structuring trust funding in a way that aligns with both your estate plan and your liquidity needs.

- Timing charitable gifts for maximum tax efficiency, which could include strategies such as gifting appreciated securities or using a donor-advised fund.

- Ensuring that business sales, real estate transactions, or other large capital events are integrated into your investment strategy in advance rather than after the fact.

When these pieces work together, you avoid missed opportunities, prevent unnecessary taxes, and reduce the risk of conflicting strategies.

Why This Matters

The payoff of true advisory work is much bigger than just a higher rate of return. It is about alignment and control. It is about knowing that every part of your financial life is working toward the same set of goals, that your plan has been stress-tested for multiple scenarios, and that you have a clear process for making decisions when the unexpected happens.

When planning, communication, and coordination are all present:

- Tax strategies are implemented intentionally instead of as last-minute fixes.

- Estate planning is kept current and aligned with your other financial decisions.

- Investment adjustments are tied to your personal situation, not to headlines or market noise.

- You have a decision-making framework that reduces stress and prevents costly mistakes.

If your current advisor does not provide this level of integration, the risk is not only in missed opportunities but also in the accumulation of small, avoidable mistakes that erode wealth over time.

Conclusion: The Future Belongs to the Flexible

The world is not standing still, and your portfolio shouldn't either. Markets shift. Tax laws evolve. Economies restructure. Your own goals, responsibilities, and opportunities change – sometimes gradually, sometimes overnight. Yet far too many portfolios remain static, built on assumptions that no longer apply or on strategies that were never aligned with your real financial life to begin with.

Throughout this book, we haven't offered a formula. We've offered a framework. A way of thinking about your investments that is grounded in intention, informed by your tax and income realities, and structured to give you control, not confusion.

Real portfolio design means recognizing that your wealth is more than a collection of accounts. It's a system that should be designed to function in your favor, across timeframes, across tax environments, and across life transitions.

Whether your next step is preparing to sell a property, consolidating old retirement accounts, stepping back from your business, or simply aligning your assets more deliberately with your life's direction, the same core principles apply:
- Be intentional with every allocation.
- Be tax-aware in every decision.
- Stay flexible enough to adapt without panic.
- And always ask: What job is this asset performing?

If you can't answer that question confidently for every part of your portfolio, you're not alone. Most investors can't. That's why a real strategy, built on clarity rather than complexity, makes such a difference.

This doesn't mean you need to change everything. Often, the most powerful shifts come from refining, not a complete overhaul. But clarity compounds just like capital does. Once you have a clear view of what you own, why you own it, and how it fits into your broader life, better decisions follow.

If your current strategy isn't aligned with that clarity, it may be time for a second opinion. Not because something is broken, but because something can work better.

Your money should serve the life you're building. Not just sit in a pie chart. Not just follow a model. Not just track a benchmark.

A real portfolio reflects real life. When you design it that way, everything shifts, from the decisions you make to the confidence you feel in making them.

Let this be the beginning of that shift.

Appendix A: Glossary of Key Terms

1031 Exchange: A tax-deferral strategy that allows real estate investors to sell one property and reinvest the proceeds into another like-kind property without immediately paying capital gains taxes.

Account Type (Taxable, IRA, Trust): The registration and tax classification of an investment account, which impacts the way income, gains, and losses are taxed.

Alternative Investments: Non-traditional assets such as private credit, hedge funds, private equity, or real estate that are used to enhance diversification or return potential.

Asset Allocation: The process of dividing investments among different categories like stocks, bonds, real estate, and alternatives to manage risk and return.

Asset Location: Strategically placing investments in taxable, tax-deferred, or tax-free accounts based on their tax characteristics.

Asymmetric Bets: Investment opportunities where the potential upside significantly outweighs the downside.

Bond Ladder: A portfolio of bonds with staggered maturities designed to provide consistent income and liquidity.

BRRR Strategy: Real estate investment strategy: Buy, Rehab, Rent, Refinance, Repeat.

Capital Efficiency: The ability of an investment to generate returns without tying up excess capital or creating unnecessary risk.

Core Portfolio: The foundational layer of a portfolio intended for long-term growth, typically made up of broadly diversified holdings.

Distribution Yield: The income (interest or dividends) distributed by an investment as a percentage of its current market price.

Dry Powder: Cash or liquid reserves kept on hand to deploy quickly when new investment opportunities or unexpected needs arise.

DST (Delaware Statutory Trust): A structure used in 1031 exchanges allowing investors to own fractional interests in institutional real estate while deferring capital gains.

ETF (Exchange-Traded Fund): A pooled investment vehicle that trades on an exchange like a stock. ETFs hold a basket of securities and provide diversification with intraday liquidity.

Family Office: A structure that manages the complete financial life of an ultra-high-net-worth family, including investments, taxes, estate, and philanthropic planning.

Income Portfolio: A section of the portfolio designed to provide stable, ongoing cash flow through dividends, interest, or rental income.

Liquidity: The ease with which an asset can be converted into cash without significantly affecting its value.

MLP (Master Limited Partnership): A business structure commonly used in energy and infrastructure that provides high distribution yields and potential tax advantages.

Position Sizing: The act of determining how much of a portfolio should be allocated to a single investment based on risk and conviction.

Preferred Stock: Hybrid security with bond-like income but some equity characteristics; senior to common stock in dividends.

Private Credit: Lending by non-bank entities, often structured as loans to private companies with higher yields and varying levels of risk.

Qualified Dividend: A dividend that meets IRS criteria for favorable tax treatment, typically taxed at long-term capital gains rates.

REIT (Real Estate Investment Trust): A company that owns or finances income-producing real estate and is required to distribute most of its income to shareholders.

Reserve Strategy: Allocating a portion of the portfolio to liquid or conservative investments to provide a buffer during market downturns or to meet cash needs.

Roth IRA: A tax-advantaged retirement account where contributions are made with after-tax dollars and qualified withdrawals are tax-free.

Tactical Allocation: Adjusting portfolio exposures in the short to medium term based on opportunities, risks, or economic outlook.

Tax Bracket: The rate at which your next dollar of income is taxed, used to assess the after-tax impact of investment income.

Tax-Loss Harvesting: Selling investments at a loss to offset capital gains elsewhere in the portfolio.

Thematic Investing: Strategy of targeting long-term macro trends (e.g., clean energy, AI, infrastructure) with focused investments.

TIPS (Treasury Inflation-Protected Securities): U.S. government bonds designed to protect against inflation. Their principal value adjusts with the Consumer Price Index, and interest is paid on the inflation-adjusted amount.

Volatility: The degree of variation in investment returns over time, often used as a proxy for risk.

Yield: Income generated by an investment, typically expressed as a percentage of the investment's current value.

Appendix B: Portfolio Self-Assessment Checklist

Ask yourself the following:

1. Does my portfolio have a purpose tied to my goals, not just growth for growth's sake?

2. Is my income plan reliable, tax-efficient, and built to last through different markets?

3. Am I using the right accounts for income and growth so I'm not overpaying in taxes?

4. Is my Roth IRA truly positioned for long-term growth, not wasted on low-return assets?

5. Have I factored real estate and private business into my overall risk and liquidity plan?

6. Are my advisor, CPA, and attorney actually working together on my behalf?

7. Do I know what a severe market downturn would mean for my portfolio and lifestyle?

8. Is my account structure and beneficiary setup up to date with my estate plan?

9. Do I have access to liquidity for opportunities or emergencies, even in volatile markets?

10. When was the last time I fully rethought my strategy to align with my current stage of life?

If you couldn't confidently answer "yes" to most of these, it may be time to evaluate your portfolio through a different lens.

About the Author

Alexis Buchholz is the founder and managing partner of BFG Wealth Management, an independent Registered Investment Advisor serving professionals, entrepreneurs, and families all with different financial lives. With over a decade of experience building custom portfolios that emphasize real-world goals, tax efficiency, and income reliability, Alexis helps clients turn abstract advice into actionable strategy.

Known for his practical approach and ability to distill complexity into clarity, Alexis wrote this book to empower investors who want more than just a generic model portfolio. He lives in Texas with his wife and four sons and serves clients across the country.

Connect

Website: www.bfgwm.com
LinkedIn: linkedin.com/in/alexisbuchholz
Email: info@bfgwm.com

Disclosures

Take the Next Step

Most portfolios are built for a generic investor. But you're not a generic investor, and your plan shouldn't be either.

If this book resonated with you, we invite you to take the next step. Whether you want a second opinion, a custom allocation strategy, or just clarity on your current structure, our team at BFG Wealth Management is here to help.

You can connect with us at **www.bfgwm.com/contact-us** to start the conversation. There's never any pressure, just the chance to bring your strategy in line with your real life.

www.ingramcontent.com/pod-product-compliance
Lightning Source LLC
Chambersburg PA
CBHW040758220326
41597CB00029BB/4983